Whispers Of The Heart

A Collection of Poems on Love

Devon Kebby

BookLeaf Publishing

India | USA | UK

Made with ❤ on the BookLeaf Publishing Platform
www.bookleafpub.in
www.bookleafpub.com

Dedication

To
My Wife, Mom, Dad, Sister, and
all my memories ...

Preface

In the depths of our souls, we harbor love for those who illuminate our lives. For things that speak to us on a profound level, and for the world around us that inspires our passions. This is "Whispers of the Heart", a collection of 21 poems, each a love letter to those who have touched our hearts.

From the radiance of a loving wife to the guidance of a mentor to the love we share with our community and nature's wild beauty, each poem in this collection tells a story of love and connection. These poems are not just expressions of love but reflections on what it means to be human.

In "Whispers of the Heart", we find ourselves in the tapestries of love, woven from threads of kindness, compassion, and self-love. We find solace in the memories that shape us, and we cherish each beat of life, for it is fleeting but precious.
This collection of poems is a testament to the power of love and connection. It is an invitation to reflect on your own relationships, and to celebrate the beauty of love in all its forms.

So let these whispers guide you on your own journey of self-discovery and love. Let them inspire you to cherish the moments that make life worth living, and to hold dear those who bring light and joy to your world.
In the words of one of our poems, "Love Thy Self", "I love the curves of my body, so unique and divine. A masterpiece crafted by nature's design." Let these words be a reminder to you, too, of your own unique beauty and the love that makes you whole.

Welcome to "Whispers of the Heart".

Acknowledgements

I would like to extend my heartfelt gratitude to those who have supported me on this journey.

First and foremost, I would like to thank my beautiful wife for being my constant source of love and inspiration. Her unwavering support and encouragement mean the world to me, and I am forever grateful for her presence in my life.
To my family, I offer my deepest appreciation. Your guidance and love have shaped me into who I am today, and I am forever in your debt.

I would also like to acknowledge the team at Bookleaf Publishing for their hard work and dedication in bringing "Whispers of the Heart" to life. Your expertise and professionalism have been a joy to work with, and I am grateful for the opportunity to share my work with a wider audience.

In addition, I would like to thank those who have inspired and influenced me throughout my life. Their thoughts, experiences, and perspectives have been invaluable to me, and I am forever changed by the time we spent together.

As I share "Whispers of the Heart" with the world, I would like to acknowledge that I have used AI services and editing tools to refine and enhance certain aspects of the poems. While the inspirations and main thoughts remain my own, I have made some modifications to ensure that the poems are polished and engaging.

I believe it is essential to be transparent about this process, as AI services can be a valuable tool in the creative process. I have used these tools to augment my own work, and I am confident that they have not compromised the authenticity of the poems.

To clarify, any modifications made to the poems using AI services are done with the intention of improving clarity, coherence, and flow. The core ideas, emotions, and themes that are central to each poem remain unchanged.

1. My Beautiful Wife

In the tapestry of your soul, I find my home,
A canvas of contrasts, where beauty is free to flow.
Not just a face, but a radiance that shines from within,
A luminescence that reaches the essence of my being.

Your mind is a symphony, a harmonious blend,
Of flaws and strengths, a brilliance no time can suspend.
In your imperfections, I find a beauty rare,
A uniqueness that makes my heart sing with profound
flair.

You're a prism of light, refracting love's pure ray,
Illuminating the path through life's joys and dismay.
In your soul's intricate dance, I find a beauty to behold,
A warm quilt of courage, heart, and gold.

You are a mystery, a riddle, a work of art divine,
A masterpiece of simplicity, with beauty that's truly
mine.
May your radiance be a reflection of the love we share,
A burning flame that guides us, through life's joys and
care.

2. Mumma I got you

She gave me life, and with it pain,
Unconditional love that will forever remain.
She wept for my mistakes, and cheered for my gains,
A constant presence that calmed life's pains.

Through trials and tribulations, she stood tall,
A rock of strength, that never would fall.
With a voice that sang both sweet and sharp refrains,
Her love, a symphony of hands that healed my pains.

Though flaws she may have, and mistakes made,
Her heart remains full of love, not a single shade.
For flaws are merely human marks, that shape a soul so
rare,
And in those flaws, your beauty shines, a love beyond
compare.

If God exists, I see it in her gentle care,
A reflection of her loving heart, always there.
I'm grateful for every sacrifice she's made to me,
A debt of love repaid, in the life our hearts will see.

3. I ain't got Daddy issues

In your eyes, a guiding light shines bright,
A beacon that leads me through life's plight.
Your selfless love and unwavering care,
Inspire me to be a better person, always fair.

Your smile, a treasure that I yearn to see,
Brings joy to my heart and sets me free.
With every passing day, I strive to make you proud,
To be the son you deserve, and never back down.

In times of doubt, when uncertainty creeps,
I seek your wisdom, and the peaceful sleep.
Your words of guidance, a treasure so rare,
Help me navigate life's twists and turns with care.

Through trials and tribulations, you stood tall,
A hero in my eyes, who bore the pain of all.
Your resilience and strength, a lesson to me,
Teach me to face challenges with courage and glee.

4. My Big Sister

Across oceans, I made a choice,
To follow your heart, my constant voice.
I left behind the familiar shore,
To chase a dream, and make you proud once more.

Your beauty shines, in every way,
A radiant soul, that lights the day.
With a new family by your side,
You tend to them with love and pride.

In times of need, my hand reaches out,
To you, dear sister, without a doubt.
You've seen me grow, through laughter and tears,
And still, you're always there, to calm my fears.

We fought as kids, with words so sharp,
But now, I look forward to a love that's from the heart.
The distance between us, may seem so vast,
But my love for you, will forever last.

5. Mentor: My Guiding Light

With gentle guidance, you helped me see,
Through clouds of confusion, clarity for me.
You soothed my fears, and gave me might,
To chase my dreams, and shine with new light.

Your words of wisdom, like a balm to me,
Soothed my doubts, and set my spirit free.
You encouraged me to take the leap of faith,
And chase my passions, with an open heart and path.

Though I may have stumbled, or sometimes been cold,
My intentions pure, my gratitude untold.
In every corner of my life, I seek your aid,
To navigate doubts, and find my way.

Your heart may be wounded, by my occasional snob,
But know that deep within me, your faith remains my
only hope.
For in your presence, I find my peaceful nest,
And with your guidance, I know I'll always be at my
best.

6. Community: The People I Call Mine

In harmony, our community stands tall,
A network of friendships that never will fall.
We weave a web of love, yet keep our space,
A delicate balance between closeness and pace.

Our bond is strong, though distance may seem wide,
We find solace in messages, words as our guide.
In group chats, our voices rise and fall,
A symphony of love that stands through it all.

Some may think us hands-off, detached and cold,
But we know better - our love is a work of gold.
For healthy relationships thrive on space and time,
A dance of closeness, yet we keep our prime.

We celebrate life's festivals with joyful sound,
And in the fire of disagreements, we're profound.
For it's in fighting that our love is refined,
A true test of friendship, where hearts entwine.

7. Nature: Whispers of the Wild

In meadows where wildflowers sway,
A symphony of whispers plays,
The rustling leaves, the gentle breeze,
Nature's unpredictable, yet always at ease.

With every step, I lose myself in her grasp,
Traversing vales where wildflowers bloom at last,
Waterfalls cascade, a symphony of sound,
My heart beats faster, my spirit unbound.

But as I wander lost in her vast domain,
I wonder what would happen if love and connection
waned,
Would I find solace in her wild, untamed heart?
Or would the emptiness of isolation tear us apart?

Yet even in difficulty, I find hope anew,
For Mother Nature's love for life will forever shine true,
Preserving the beauty of our world, a treasure rare,
And filling my heart with love that's never gone.

8. Books: Love between the Pages

In childhood's days, the pages lay unturned,
Yet seeds of curiosity took root within.
With time and tech, a map I drew to find,
A path through libraries where the stories bind.

From soft whispers to hard-hitting truths,
Diverse genres filled my mind with new views.
Each story's depth, each character's roots,
A newfound love for tales of every kind.

Through tales of kings and ancient lore,
In histories wrapped in fiction's gentle score.
I found the love I missed before,
In every story's warm and timeless roar.

Be it physical or digital hues,
The joy of reading never fades;
I share this joy with all who choose
To pause and turn life's hurried page.

9. Music: Notes to My Soul

In childhood's quiet nights, I'd strain to hear the sound,
Melodies through walls, in neighbors' homes softly
spread around.
The distant tunes would call, a siren to my ear,
Community's embrace brought music ever near.

With cassette tapes, new songs unveiled their charm,
I sang along, disturbing peace at home by clamor.
Yet in those tunes, my spirit never failed to thrive,
For music made the world my own sweet dome.

These notes have been my friends, companions of the
soul,
In harmonies and chords, I've found myself whole.
The music and its love, forever intertwined,
A soundtrack to my life, the essence of my mind.

In jazz's soft refrains and gentle beats, I find my place,
A love for music that forever will not fade or lose its
pace.
Through changing times, it holds me fast and true,
A friendship pure that helped me grow.

10. Art: Colors of my Heart

In the brushstrokes of a visionary's hand,
I find solace in the colors of my land.
From Pablo's Cubists to Nature's own design,
Art is a language that speaks directly to mine.

With every stroke, a piece of me is set free,
A manifestation of emotions, for all to see.
Art's the voice that speaks when words cannot say,
A universal language, that reaches far and wide each
day.

In nature's canvas, art flows with the breeze,
A masterpiece unrivaled and unrolled.
The song of wind through ancient trees,
Speaks in whispers through the night, a symphony of
ease.

When voices fade in tyranny's dark night,
Through art, the soul finds strength to break anew.
Silent tales they tell, whispers within every stroke,
Art reveals the heart, and life and love in colors spoke.

11. Home: Where the Heart Always Returns

In spaces crafted, where heart finds rest,
A refuge from the world's din and unrest.
I design an atmosphere of peace and light,
Where growth, comfort, and joy entwine in sight.

No need to prove or wear a mask,
In my sanctuary, I am free to embark.
Chores and tasks become a part of me,
As I nurture soul and a peaceful energy.

This haven shifts with life's design,
Yet familiar beauty stays inside.
I roam, yet this essence makes each place my home,
Where I am myself, without a single tome.

In this sacred space, my heart yearns to be,
Free from tests and doubts, where love shines free.
If you don't feel the same love and care,
Perhaps you're in someone else's home, unaware.

12. Work: The Grind I Cherish

In dawn's early light, I rise with zeal,
To tackle my grind, and seize the day to feel real
A sense of pride, a heart full of stride,
As I labor hard, my soul's delight.

Beyond the paycheck's mundane call,
I find a purpose worth fighting for, standing tall.
Not just means to keep lights bright,
But passion burning through the night.

With each dawn, a new day's birth,
I face challenges with a willing heart.
My mind and soul entwine, in tasks so divine,
Where every task is a step, a climb to shine.

In labor that ignites my mind,
I touch the lives of humankind, a love so kind.
The grind I cherish every day,
A source of joy that fuels my way.

13. Dreams: Chasing the Infinite

As a child, I reached for the stars,
Astronaut was my first celestial scar.
I chased that dream, with a curious mind,
And found myself flying, leaving fears behind.

Years went by, and new dreams took hold,
To pilot the skies, with a spirit bold.
I trained hard, with sweat and with tears,
And found my passion, through all the passing years.

I changed cities, countries, continents too,
Embracing cultures diverse, with an open heart anew.
I made my parents proud, and lived up to the test,
And now I stand, where once I only dreamed my best.

Loving each dream, for the fire it ignites,
Ambitions soar, as I set my sights.
I had a dream, that drove me to succeed,
And now it's all within reach, my heart's greatest need.

14. Travel: Love in Every Mile

As I look back, travel was a test,
A chore of plans and luggage unrest,
But parents' love and gentle might,
Set me free to explore, day and night.

In dawns that stretched across the land,
I chased sunrises with an open hand,
Each place a mirror, clear and bright,
Reflecting facets of my inner light.

With age, the fire that burned so bright,
Faded into embers of delightful sight,
But now I yearn for wanderlust's thrill,
To rediscover the world, and my inner will.

Now every mile holds a story new,
In each journey lies a heart that's true,
Traveling sets the soul free to roam,
And in its freedom, I find my heart's home.

15. Love Thy Self

In mirrors deep, my eyes behold
A story of myself untold,
Embracing all I am inside,
With self-love as my trusted guide.

I love the curves of my body, so unique and divine,
A masterpiece crafted by nature's design.
My personality shines bright, a work of art that's mine,
A reflection of my soul, where love and light entwine.

With hands that create and a mind that dares,
I stand firm, unshaken by the stares,
My journey, a tapestry, rich and vast,
Woven with threads that I hold dear, at last.

To the world, I bring my pride and grace,
In my work, I leave a lasting trace,
Inspiring hearts to rise, to shine, to be,
Loving myself, and inspiring all to be free.

16. My Future Child: A Love Yet to Be

In your eyes, a future unfurls,
Unbound by expectations' bounds and curls.
Free to soar, your dreams will take flight,
And shine with a light that guides us through the night.

Your path, I wish to see you carve with ease,
Beyond the limitations that society pleases.
Let your ambitions soar, untethered and high,
And know that success and failure are but a sigh.

With confidence, you'll face the skies,
And inspire others as your spirit flies.
For in self-love and trust, you'll find your way,
To become the author of your own destiny's sway.

We are rooted, branches intertwined with care,
Growing in our own way, yet forever connected there.
You are me, and your mother, a love that's true,
Promising to love you more than myself, forever shining
through.

17. Memories: The Keeper of Time

In whispers soft, my memories reside,
Grounding me deep, a consistent tide.
Bringing back the beauty of days gone by,
Laughter and love beneath the sky.

I cherish these moments, both old and new,
Guiding my steps, as a path anew.
Regrets and lessons learned, a valuable pack,
Teaching resilience, with each passing track.

Some memories shine like sunshine in my eyes,
While others carry weight, of mistakes and sighs.
Yet even those, hold value in their own way,
A lesson learned, to guide me through the day.

These memories are the keepers of our past,
Holding joys and sorrows, that forever will last.
To forget them is to lose a part of me,
Unlucky are those who abandon their memories.

18. Teachers: Lessons Beyond the Classroom

In hallowed halls where knowledge grows,
They light the path that wisdom shows.
With every lesson, roots run deep,
Their guiding words my soul will keep.

From academic paths to character's might,
They instilled in me the values of day and night,
Unconventional methods, a treasure to see,
Helping me grow in diverse ways, wild and free.

With honesty clear, their wisdom shone,
Admitting when old truths were gone.
They urged me to question, to seek and explore,
To nurture my mind and learn evermore.

With every step, a path was lit,
Their legacy lives on, a treasure rare and bright,
A debt of gratitude I'll forever share,
In their unapologetic ways, my heart is aware.

With every step, their light still shines,
A legacy etched in endless lines.

A debt of gratitude I'll always bear,
For lessons that shaped me beyond compare.

19. Life: A Love Eternal

In the tapestry of time, a gem is born,
Life's preciousness, forever sworn.
With seconds to destroy, yet months to create,
It takes our breath, a miracle to relate.

From peaks so high to valleys wide,
Love's gentle light will be our guide.
In every heartbeat, a story unfolds,
A legacy woven, as moments grow old.

The whispers of wisdom, life imparts with care,
Guiding us through the ages, beyond compare.
With each breath I take, my spirit feels whole,
In the depth of gratitude, my soul takes its role.

In love with life, I cherish each beat,
A rhythm that makes my world complete.
A fleeting spark, yet endlessly bright,
A thread that weaves both day and night.

20. Time: Fleeting but Precious

In the dance of hours, I weave a life so fine,
Each tick, each tock, a precious beat that's mine.
Like coins in a purse, each second I carefully store,
An inventory of laughter, both waking and sleep's score.

With purpose, I measure the tides of my days,
Assimilating wisdom in bright sun's rays.
Attention bestowed, I refine each pursuit with care,
Efficiency blossoms as I plant mindful roots to share.

Memories, like letters penned in the dark of night,
Chronicles radiant, igniting a spark to ignite.
Each hour a treasure, an essence to impart,
Marking milestones, love written in the fabric of time's
heart.

So I cradle this time, my heart interlaced with care,
In the ledger of living, where all hope is faced and
shared.
For in valuing moments, transformation takes flight,
In the flow of time, my soul's purest light shines bright.

21. Humanity: The Heart of Us All

In the depths of humanity's soul,
A bond so strong, it makes us whole.
Unite our hearts with kindness true,
And guide us through the darkest night anew.

When storms of fate come crashing down,
We answer duty's urgent call, unbound.
With open hearts and spirits free,
We find our kinship, wild and glee.

Compassion's flame, within us held,
Burns bright and steady, never quelled.
It guides us through the winding path,
Where love and duty never clash.

In humankind's heart, a flame burns bright,
Compassion's answer to suffering pain and night.
With every touch, a gentle, helping hand,
We find our purpose, in this human land.

www.ingramcontent.com/pod-product-compliance
Lightning Source LLC
LaVergne TN
LVHW021345200726
843509LV00014B/2673